The
Libra Personality

Understanding Your Own
Innate Libra Personality
Traits and Libra
Characteristics to Become
a Better Libra Woman

by Aviana Burton

Table of Contents

Introduction

Did you know that as a Libra woman, you have specific and innate personality traits that are unique from all other Zodiac signs? The Libra disposition tends to be a balanced personality with a great deal of hidden potential. If you're a Libra, there's a lot more to yourself that you may not even know, mainly because it's buried much deeper than surface level characteristics.

By delving into these exclusive characteristics and personality traits (including not only your strengths, but also your weaknesses) you will be able to better leverage them for your own advantage, thereby optimizing your chances for success in the various areas of life.

Now of course, harnessing your Libra personality traits to become a better woman is easier said than done, and it will take a scientific approach and a set of properly planned-out steps in order to accomplish this. Each enhancement you choose to undertake must be attuned to your personality as a Libra in order for you to triumph over the adversities.

This book will help you to better understand the very nature of your astrological sign, and it will teach you how to nurture and apply the positive Libra traits while correcting and compensating for the negative ones. It will provide you with concrete steps you can conveniently implement so that you can explore the inner-workings of your astrological personality and grow and evolve into a better and more mature Libra woman.

What are you waiting for? Let's get started!

Chapter 1: Understanding Your Innate Libra Personality Traits

The Libra individual is one of the most interesting Zodiac personalities. A combination of your astrology, the ruling planet placement, your element and your sun sign influence what you can be as a person. However, these comprise only a portion of your persona; what you do with these Zodiac aspects is the primary driving force that can allow you to succeed in life.

This means that your destiny will depend not only on your stars, but primarily on what you do with what the stars give you. One of the lines of the famous Shakespearean play, Julius Caesar, goes like this: *"The fault, dear Brutus, is not in our stars, but in ourselves."* This means that you have to do something positive about your traits for you to prosper in life.

Basic facts that will help you understand:

1. Libra women don't have identical traits

Libras possess general traits but are never identical. This will depend on the placement of their planets. Some may have Mars or Venus. For simplicity, the sun sign is used in these discussions. Nevertheless, take note that there are major traits that you have just like the other Librans.

2. Librans are born in September or October

Librans are people who are born between September 23 and October 22 in any year. It's the 7th of the Zodiac signs.

3. The major traits of a Libran are Inner calmness and balance

This is the major trait of Librans in both genders. They are individuals who decry conflict and confrontation and would go to great lengths to maintain peace and harmony.

4. Libra women have more positive traits than other Zodiac signs

You're lucky you're a Libran because among all the Zodiac signs, Libra women have the most positive traits. So you can maximize these to convert your perceived losses into victories.

5. Libra women like the following:

- Meeting new people—They enjoy gaining new friends and acquaintances.

- Partying—They love partying, spending time and having fun with friends.

- Harmony—There has to be harmony between things around them.

- New adventures—They also like to experience new adventures and do new things. Change is a great event for them.

- Talking—They like to talk a lot, and they relish being the center of attention.

Knowing more about and being aware of your personality can help you in your pursuit of becoming the person you want to be.

12

Chapter 2: Nurturing the Positive Characteristics

As previously mentioned, your positive traits as a Libra woman surpass that of all the other Zodiac signs. How lucky! BUT (and this is a big "but"), if you don't know how to take advantage of these positive traits, they're useless. So, how can you nurture your positive characteristics?

Step #1—Know your positive traits

The first step is to know what these positive characteristics are. How can you nurture your traits if you don't know them? The Zodiac sign for a Libran is a scale because Librans are generally balanced personalities; they don't go to extremes. These are the specific positive Libran traits.

- **Balanced**—She weighs the possible outcomes of anything she encounters and stays at the middle to maintain balance. She's never too caught up in any idea that harbor extreme notions.

- **Optimistic**—She typically looks forward to the positive things in life and is hopeful that everything will turn out well.

- **Easy-going**—She's easy to be with and can get along with almost anyone. She can adjust easily to the behaviors of other people.

- **Natural leader**—People usually select her as the leader because without being aware of it, the Libra woman leads her group.

- **Diplomatic**—A Libra woman can be a great negotiator and mediator.

- **Peacemaker**—She solves problems utilizing peaceful solutions

- **Charismatic**—She naturally charms people. Libra women are mostly physically beautiful, and for those who are not perfect physically, they make use of their charm to attract people. This makes her a good politician, teacher, lecturer, religious leader or someone of a similar occupation.

- **Amiable**—She can easily make friends because of her amiable personality. Since she does not discriminate, she associates with new people quickly.

- **Persuasive**—She can be persuasive when she chooses to be, persuading people to her side in issues that need to be resolved.

- **Self-confident**—She's self-confident and can hold her own in any group. This is due to the fact that she knows her true worth.

- **Kind**—She is kind to everyone, and sees to it that no one is maltreated or discriminated against.

- **Elegant**—She displays elegance and grace when carrying herself. She has good fashion sense and is able to exude character in her fashion style.

- **Sociable**—She can mingle in a crowd without becoming self-conscious, and feels comfortable whether being left alone amidst people, or left alone at home. She's more of an extrovert, one who loves being with friends, colleagues and family.

- **Quick-witted**—She is smart and can hold a conversation with her quick wit and amiability. You can expect an intelligent conversation with a Libra woman.

- **Sense of justice**—She values justice when dealing with other people. If she feels that someone is treated unkindly or unjustly, she will mediate and see to it that justice is served for that person.

- **Intelligent**—She is intelligent. Some may not have genius IQs but they're street smart and wise in many ways.

- **Artistic**—She loves the arts and music, and enjoys things of beauty. You can see her visiting an art gallery, attending a beauty pageant or a concert.

- **Hardworking**—She works with dedication and commitment. She doesn't stop until she finishes a task. She's usually the first to report to work and last to leave.

Step #2—Make a conscious effort to apply your positive traits

Now that you know the positive characteristics of a Libra woman, you can focus on nurturing and developing them. Believe that you possess these traits and you just have to allow them to show. This signifies that you have to be self-confident that you have them. It should be a conscious choice and a determined one. In any given situation, apply whatever trait is required. It's not enough that you know of their innate existence, you have to make a conscious effort to practice and apply them.

An example is when you're tasked to brainstorm about new projects in your career; you should consciously act as the leader because you know that innately, you are a leader. Some Libra women are late bloomers; they don't realize their strengths until someone points it out to them, or when they become aware that they have a strong trait deep inside of them.

Another example is when you're at a party and you don't know what to do. Remember that you have the innate ability to socialize and make friends quickly. Nurture this trait by actually coming out of your shell and interacting with people at the party. You have the required trait to do this, so why limit yourself by not acknowledging that you have it?

All you have to do now is develop all your positive traits as a Libra woman and nurture them through constant application. You have to tap into them yourself and allow them to evolve and be expressed through your actions.

Step #3—Practice, practice, practice these positive traits

It's unwise to think that since you already have these innate traits, you can quickly apply them. Perhaps with some traits you can, but traits or characteristics are just like muscles, you have to exercise or practice them so that they can become evident. The muscles are there, but if you don't exercise them, they won't grow and develop strength. Hence, you have to practice using your good traits whenever the occasion allows it. Learning is retention and application, and practice, practice, practice.

These are the three simple steps to nurture your positive characteristics. You can allow all these traits to appear at the forefront, if you believe you have them, and hone them to make you into a better woman.

Chapter 3: How to Apply, Optimize, and Reinforce Your Qualities

The positive traits mentioned in Chapter 2 are useless if you don't utilize them. Here are specific instances in which you can do so.

Specific traits and instances in which you can use these traits

- **Balanced**

   As mentioned, you're a balance personality, so don't harbor extreme ideas because this will go against your inner self and can cause problems. Instead, build a strong foundation around this good trait by consciously balancing the pros and cons of events or things before arriving at a final decision.

- **Optimistic**

You can use your optimism during times that people around you are depressed. A specific example is when your brother has been fired from work; you can share your positive thoughts with him. Tell him that "Everything happens for a reason," what he is suffering at present may be an open door for him to find a more rewarding job.

You can also share the success story of how Kentucky Fried Chicken (KFC) came to be because the owner persisted in knocking at the doors of a hundred houses. There are various ways you can use your optimism to help people. "If you think you can, then you can." Let this trait work to your advantage. People will like to be around you when you light up the room with your positive behavior. This will have a beneficial impact on your career, home and relationships.

- **Easy-going**

You can use this trait when relating to people around you. When you're an easy-going person, you don't find fault with others, you are jovial and easy to approach. Practice this behavior in your office or place of work and people will love being around you.

- **Sense of justice**

Report to the proper authorities any injustice you witness. Be aware that your inner self doesn't like injustice. So if you witness an incident of injustice, don't hesitate to ask for help; because if you don't, you'll forever feel guilty about the incident. This guilt can fester in your soul and destroy your future dealings with people.

- **Love for the arts**

If you feel like visiting an art gallery or listening to a piano recital, you should take time and spare some money for it. Don't be reluctant because you're also nurturing that positive trait. After all, not everyone has such a heightened sense for all things aesthetical.

- **Charisma**

There will be instances when you feel inferior or ugly. Don't feel this way, because inside you is a charismatic person. You can charm even a snake if you recognize this and hone this superb trait. How? By telling yourself that you have charm, and acting that way. Being charismatic is not acquired overnight; it's a trait that is acquired through practice.

- **Natural leader**

When you're in doubt of your ability to lead, remember that you're a natural leader. Throw all your doubts into the wind and stand tall. Volunteer to lead your team, spearhead a movement, or create groups on your own. You already have that trait, you just have to bring it out and believe in yourself.

- **Diplomacy**

Use this in times when a person confronts you or talks back at you. When this happens, follow these steps:

1. Invite the person respectfully to sit down.

2. Introduce yourself and ask him to identify himself/herself (if you don't know the person yet).

3. Ask him his purpose.

4. Clarify his purpose by asking questions, such as "So, did you come here to find out why you weren't promoted?"

5. Once his purpose is clear, present the facts.

6. Allow him to understand the facts clearly.

7. Ask him what he would have done in that incident, if he were in your shoes.

8. Listen to what he has to say.

9. Compromise. If this is not possible, then you have to try to let the person feel how it is to be in your shoes.

Diplomacy is a skill, and learning the ropes can take a long time. Since you have it within you, with persistence, you can eventually perfect the skill.

• **Peacemaker**

Becoming a peacemaker is similar to practicing diplomacy. When mediating between two "warring" groups or individuals, you have to listen to both sides. Jot down your observations and conclusions, so you can refer to them in the future in clarifying statements. You have to have at least two witnesses to the proceedings. You can use these steps.

1. Arrange a meeting between the two groups.

2. Allow each group to present its side. You can establish rules during the presentation that no one should interrupt; no shouting; no cuss words; and that everybody should listen.

3. Summarize the presentation of each group by focusing on the main points.

4. An open discussion follows where questions are asked and answered observing proper decorum.

5. Both groups present their solutions to the issues raised.

6. A compromise is agreed upon by both groups. Don't give your own suggestions, just guide them while they themselves provide the answer.

Being a peacemaker in major misunderstandings can be a Herculean task, but with practice, you can hone your innate ability. You can even use this as your instrument to achieve greater heights in your career.

In trifle incidences, you just have to act as the mediator for both parties to come to a compromise that would be mutually beneficial.

- **Amiability**

You can nurture your amiability by believing in your ability to make people like you.

Approach people with a smile and allow them to talk about themselves. Provide some help if necessary. An example is when you have new employees in your office. Be the first to greet and welcome them. Invite them for lunch or coffee breaks. Don't ignore them. Be of help if they aren't familiar with something in your office. Amiability is simply being a friend to people around you.

- **Persuasiveness**

Your persuasive trait is good when you want someone to think the way you do. If you're a salesperson, you can easily sell your products through persuasion. How can you do this? By knowing all about the product you're selling. Know the facts about the item or event. Don't rely on rumors or hearsay to convince another person. You have to know the facts and provide evidence of these facts. If you can do this, your persuasive trait is being developed positively. Hence, if you're selling, present the facts about the product. Present personal reviews or affirmations from customers who have used the product.

- **Self-confidence**

You can boost your self-confidence to the way it should be by applying the cybernetics law—act self-confident and you'll soon acquire the trait. If you don't feel the confidence now, don't fret. It's there waiting to be brought to the forefront. How can you nurture self-confidence? Here are some actions you can take:

1. Act confident by standing with your back straight, and your chin up.

2. When speaking, avoid using words such as "maybe", "perhaps", "I don't know", and "I'm not sure."

3. Use positive verbs, such as, "will", "can" and confident terms, such as "certainly" and "absolutely".

4. Maintain eye contact and speak loud and clear.

5. Don't fidget or give in to distracting mannerisms, such as pulling your hair, playing with your fingers or stamping your feet.

You can also develop your self-confidence steadily by constantly visualizing yourself acting confidently.

- **Kindness**

You can develop this trait through simple actions in your daily life. Be kind to the old woman crossing the street, by assisting her to cross. Be kind to the lost dog by providing a shelter. Be kind to the hungry teen in your block by helping him find a part time job. There are numerous ways to be kind to people.

- **Elegance**

You can display elegance through your choice of clothing and the way you hold yourself. Maintain your poise and elegance even during trying situations. When someone shouts at you in public, show your elegance by not stooping to that level. Select clothes that are age appropriate. If you're over 50, you should not avoid clothes, such as midriffs and mini-skirts, which are for teens. Racy dresses are also not recommended. How can you appear elegant if a part of your boob is peeking through your dress? Elegance involves both your behavior and your appearance.

• **Sociability**

Cultivate this trait by going out with family, friends and colleagues. Circulate around and get to know people during parties. Don't be a wall-flower. It's not your style. Allow the hibernating larva to hatch into the social butterfly that you truly are. Dance, interact, and participate in activities created for the event. Tap into your amiability to practice this trait.

• **Quick-wittedness**

Wit is also a skill that can be honed through practice. In order to do this, you have to be a wide-reader. Continuously acquiring knowledge will allow you to react quickly during conversations. Read about current events and what's trending today. Newspapers, TV, and the Internet are good sources for acquiring information on daily events. Make it a habit to read the news for the day before proceeding to your daily activities. You should also widen your vocabulary by reading books. Read fiction and other informative books.

- **Hard-worker**

Librans are naturally hard-workers. If you have not recognized this trait in you, you can develop it by becoming a dedicated worker in any task that you're assigned to. A dedicated worker is output oriented, ready to complete tasks without slacking. Avoid looking at the clock until you have finished what was set for the day.

- **Intelligence**

Intelligence can be enhanced through studying and reading, as well. If you're a student, you have to pay attention to lectures and then try to understand them more through studying. Use the Internet discriminately to gain more knowledge. You can also develop your musical intelligence by learning how to play musical instruments. Exercise your mind's cognitive ability by playing memory games or word games.

These are specific ways to enrich your innate traits. Implement them and gain the essential benefits from these activities.

Chapter 4: Correcting and Improving the Negative Characteristics

On the other hand, you also have negative traits just like any other person. The good news is that you don't have to give in to these shortcomings but you can improve them instead for your own benefit.

Step #1—Know your negative traits

What are these negative traits that you must be aware of? If you know them, then you can avoid or conquer them. Generally, a Libra woman has these negative characteristics:

- **Demanding**—She demands attention, and she tends to be bossy, so she will keep demanding things from other people just to satisfy her focus on details.

- **Flirtatious**—She can be a flirt at times because of her beauty and charm. But she's just having a good time trying to see how far her charms can work for her.

- **Unreliable**—Because of her attention to detail, she tends to be unreliable in keeping up with deadlines. At times, she may not be able to come on time for meetings or dates.

- **Don't know how to say "no"**—She is kind, up to a fault that she has difficulty saying "no." As long as she can do it, she will always say "yes."

- **Obsession with details**—She concentrates on details to the extent that the significance of the whole picture is often neglected. She also nitpicks because of her obsession with details.

- **Pushover**—Because of her extreme kindness and conciliatory attitude, she may appear to be a pushover.

- **Indecisive**—This is also the effect of being very kind and peace loving. She becomes indecisive because she considers everyone's benefit.

- **Vain**—She is too conscious of her appearance, and will look at the mirror more often than the majority of women do. Since she wants elegance and beauty, she will overindulge in her fashion and physical appearance.

Step #2—Strive to correct these negative traits

Since you're now aware of these negative traits, you can consciously do something about them. When you feel them surfacing in your behavior, put your foot down and don't allow them to.

An example is when you notice that you're about to say "yes" to a request that doesn't concern you, pause for a few minutes and say "no" instead.

Another one is when you're working on a task and you keep repeating it because you're obsessing about the details; pause for a while and evaluate the major objective of the task. If what you have done has fulfilled the goal of the task, then you have to stop focusing on the insignificant details.

Chapter 5: Becoming a Better Libra Woman, Step-by-Step

Your good Libra traits are numerous and through them, you can become a better person. How can you use them? Here are simple and easy steps you can follow.

Steps #1—Evaluate yourself

On a piece of paper, evaluate your strong and weak traits. List your strong points on the right and your weak points on the left. Be truthful so that this exercise can be helpful. Maintain your strong points, and keep cultivating them.

Step #2—Beside your weak traits, list what you can do to eliminate them

The things you plan to do must be specific and doable, and should correct the negative characteristic. An example is the "Action Table" on the next page.

Negative traits	Action Taken	Results
Demanding	Starting from today, I will stop demanding that a colleague must wait for me during lunch time.	Succeeded in eating lunch with whoever was free.
Flirtatious	I won't do suggestive acts of flirting when I'm with men, such as licking my lips or shaking my booty.	Failed once, must keep on trying.
Unreliable	I won't be late for appointments or deadlines.	Late twice for a total of 6 deadlines.
Don't know how to say "no"	I'll say "no" to requests that I find difficult to fulfill, such as helping others with their tasks when I haven' finished mine yet.	Haven't succeeded YET; will try harder.
Obsession with details	I won't focus on the details of the group assignment but on the goals.	Bit by bit, I'm learning. I'll do it again next week.
Pushover	I won't give in, if the request inconveniences me.	No success yet, will keep trying.
Indecisive	When I say "no", I won't budge or be swayed.	No success either. I'm not giving up
Vain	I will look at the mirror only thrice a day.	Yahoo! I've succeeded.

You can prepare a table for each week, so that you can easily monitor your progress. Remember, the speed in which you can turn around your negative traits will depend on your awareness, determination and perseverance. Keep trying, you haven't failed as long as you keep trying.

Step #3—After a month, evaluate your progress

After a month of implementing the actions you have specified, evaluate your progress by perusing the tables of your actions that you have documented for the past month. From the results, you can change the "action taken" if you have already succeeded in correcting or eliminating that particular negative trait. Nevertheless, you still have to keep tabs on these negative traits because they might resurface again when you're not thinking of them.

Step #4—Keep the cycle going

Try to keep the cycle of correcting your unwanted traits every month. Some may be difficult to eliminate, but be patient. You have to record all your actions to be able to do this. Eventually, you will succeed through this method.

There's always room for improvement. Take note that the only permanent thing in this world is change. If you follow this method, you will indeed be able to change for the better. By knowing your negative traits, you can correct them to become a more fulfilled individual.

Chapter 6: Finding Love and Fostering Romance

The Libra woman has the most lovable traits that some people don't appreciate. As a Libra, you must also learn how to appreciate your self-worth. You should also know what Zodiac signs are considered the most compatible partners for you. Here are some pointers in the area of romance.

As a Libra woman, your best matches are Aquarius and Gemini. Men who have these Zodiac signs complement your personality well. If these signs are not available, you can choose an Aries, Virgo or Libra, as well. Below are the details of the Zodiac signs that are compatible with you in the area of romance. This list is arranged in the order in which they're most compatible with you.

1. **Aquarius**

An Aquarius man is one of the best partners for you. This is due to the fact that your personalities complement each other. You will have several common traits with an Aquarian, such as being sociable, friendly and having a love for adventure and something new.

2. Gemini

You can live comfortably and happily with a Gemini man because you can be similar in certain traits but also have some variation. This is the perfect formula for lasting marriages. A Gemini is also an extrovert, who loves being with friends and meeting new ones. But he's not as kind as you, so this trait will be tempered with his intervention.

3. Libra

A relationship with another Libra is good but not as excellent as that with an Aquarius or Gemini. Since both of you have similar traits, you like the same things and enjoy the same hobbies. You're both diplomatic; you both love beauty, peace, harmony, and the arts, and you want new adventures in your life. The setback is that, this can be boring at times, because you may find things too familiar.

4. Virgo

The Virgo is a perfectionist, which is similar to your focus on details. He's also independent and calm, just as you are. He can help you with your unreliability because he's a reliable person, someone you can depend on when it comes to deadlines. Hence, you can have a good relationship with a Virgo.

5. Aries

The Aries male is self-confident and loves adventure. He can be spontaneous and brazen at times, and just like you, he is vain. He can happily agree with you to seek out new things to do. Watch out for his temper though, because the Aries male has a tendency to become violent.

While males from the other Zodiac signs are not recommended as a good partner for you, of course, you can always choose from the other signs if you truly love the man. Choosing your life partner from the above compatible signs is, however, more likely to lead to a meaningful, lasting and fulfilling relationship.

Chapter 7: Additional Pointers for Being a Libra Woman

Being a Libra woman is the best card that you have. You have to play your card right and use all your potential to triumph over all adversities and become a better person. To help in this quest, here are important tips to bear in mind.

1. **Don't spend too much money on your appearance.** Physical appearance matters, but what matters more is your inner beauty. Your inner beauty will always shine through, so focus more on that.

2. **As a Libra woman, you can be successful as a writer, teacher, actress, artist and lawyer.** You can also thrive as a diplomat or a politician with your intellect, sense of justice, charm and wit.

3. **In other calendars, the Zodiac sign Libra includes the days from September 23 to October 23.** However, the most common is up to October 22.

4. **Your favorable months are January, February, March, July, September, November, and December.** The rest are unfavorable. Hence, you can plan your major activities around these months.

5. **Commonly, Librans are ruled by the planet Venus.** This means that in love, you tend to be a romantic, loving harmony and peace in a relationship. Librans don't believe in the acute thrills of "love at first sight" but tend to be more comfortable with relationships that occur in a "peaceful" environment.

6. **A positive trait can turn into a negative trait.** So, be aware of this. An example is kindness. Too much kindness may not be good also for the recipient of your act. He may depend on your kindness for life and won't strive to become independent.

7. **Your lucky numbers are 6, 15, 24, 33, 51 and 60.** You may want to use them whenever necessary.

8. **Your birthstone or lucky stone is opal.** Experts in the Zodiac signs believe that if you wear your birthstone, it will bring luck to your undertakings, so, you may want to wear a necklace or bracelet with an opal stone.

9. **Casual affairs are not favored by Librans.** Therefore, don't jump into these relationships because in the long run, you won't like it at all. Your innate character loves relationships that are lasting and meaningful.

10. **These Libra traits can be influenced by your environment.** Even if you have these innate traits, if you don't make your environment conducive to the development of these traits, you won't be making the most of them.

11. **Your success depends not solely on your innate traits.** It also depends on how you use them. Use them wisely to do well.

Together with the information provided in the other chapters, these are some of the pointers that you can observe as a Libra woman to advance in your career and prosper in relationships.

Conclusion

The Libra woman is a woman endowed with much potential and many good traits. You can either use them to become a better person or just allow them to be there without enhancing them. Your destiny in life does not only depend on your innate Libra characteristics but also on all factors around you. The ability to use all of these factors in your environment to turn your life into your dream is all in your hands.

Use the information that you have gleaned here wisely and you won't regret it. Just keep in mind that your choices and actions today will surely influence what you will be in the future. You're a Libra woman, who loves peace, harmony and beauty, and you should be proud of it.

As for your negative traits, you have your whole life to get rid of them or turn them into "lemonade." You can become a better woman by starting NOW!

Finally, I'd like to thank you for purchasing this book! If you enjoyed it or found it helpful, I'd greatly appreciate it if you'd take a moment to leave a review on Amazon. Thank you!